The Little Baseball Poetry Book

The Little Baseball Poetry Book

Walter the Educator

Silent King Books

CONTENTS

CONTENTS

CONTENTS

dedicated to all the baseball lovers in the world

Diamond Glows

The diamond glows with evening light,
The crowd is hushed, a sacred rite.
The pitcher winds, the batter poised,
The crack of wood, the crowd rejoiced.

The ball soars high into the sky,
The outfielders begin to fly.
They race, they run, they reach and leap,
The ball falls in, the crowd will keep.

The game is long, the pace is slow,
The tension builds with each new throw.
The pitcher tires, the batter waits,
The game is won with home plate's gates.

The cheers go up, the players smile,
The game is over, but for a while,
The memories linger, the stories told,
The game of baseball, never grows old.

Rules and the Plays
Intertwine

The crack of the bat, the roar of the crowd,
The game of baseball, where rules abound.
From strikes to balls, to base hits and steals,
Each play has a purpose, each moment appeals.
The pitcher winds up, the ball leaves his hand,
The batter takes aim, hoping to grandstand.
A swing and a miss, a strike one is called,
The count starts to build, the tension is enthralled.
Three strikes you're out, the umpire will say,
But four balls you walk, to first base you'll stay.
The game has its rules, its strategies too,
From bunting to stealing, there's much to pursue.
The outfielders roam, ready to catch,
The infielders stay put, waiting to snatch.
A ground ball, a pop-up, a fly to deep right,
Each play has its moment, each player in sight.
The game of baseball, a true American pastime,

Where the rules and the plays intertwine.
From Little League to the majors, it's a game we all love,
With each pitch and each swing, we can't get enough.

Fields of Green

In fields of green, where summers reign,
The players gather to begin the game,
Their bats held tight, their gloves at the ready,
As the crowd cheers on, loud and heady.
The pitcher takes his place on the mound,
His eyes locked in, his focus profound,
He winds and throws with speed and might,
The ball soaring through the air in flight.
The batter stands with steady grace,
Waiting for the ball to find its place,
His swing is quick, his aim is true,
A home run hit, the crowd in a hue.
The fielders run and leap with glee,
Catching pop flies and grounders with ease,
Their teamwork strong, their spirits high,
As they play the game beneath the sky.
And when the game is done and won,
The players smile, proud of all they've done,

For baseball is more than just a game,
It's a passion, a love, an eternal flame.

Managers and Coaches

In baseball, there are managers and coaches,
Guiding the team, helping them reach for the roses.
They strategize and plan, with every pitch and swing,
Hoping to lead their team to a championship ring.
The managers are the leaders, the ones in charge,
Making tough decisions, never faltering or barge.
They motivate and inspire, always pushing for more,
Ensuring their team is ready for whatever's in store.
The coaches are the teachers, the ones who refine,
Helping players perfect their craft, every single time.
They work on technique, form, and skill,
Making sure each player is ready to fulfill.
Together, they form a team, a force to be reckoned,
Working tirelessly, never resting or second-guessing.
With passion and dedication, they lead their team,
Hoping to achieve the ultimate baseball dream.
So here's to the managers and coaches in this game,
For their hard work and commitment, we say your name.

We celebrate your efforts, your passion, and your drive,
For without you, baseball would not thrive.

Warriors of the Game

In black and white, they stand so tall,
Majestic as the game unfolds.
Their calls can make or break it all,
In the game of baseball, they hold.

With eagle eyes, they watch each throw,
The strikes, the balls, the fouls, the hits.
Their judgments make the players know,
If they should stay or call it quits.

They face the wrath of angry fans,
Of coaches, players, and the press.
But they still do what they can,
To make the game a fair success.

They're umpires, warriors of the game,
Whose honor lies in what they do.
And though they may not always claim fame,
They're heroes to the baseball crew.

Locked In

The pitcher on the mound,
With the ball in his hand,
He thinks of all the strategies,
To strike out the opposing band.

The batter at the plate,
Eyes locked on the ball,
He plans his swing with precision,
To make the pitcher fall.

The fielders in their places,
Ready for the ball to fly,
They know their roles and duties,
To catch the ball on the fly.

The runners on the bases,
Eager to take their lead,
They watch and wait for the moment,
To steal and succeed.

The game of baseball strategy,
Is an art like no other,

It takes skill, practice, and patience,
To win and conquer.
    But in the end, the team that prevails,
Is the one that plays with heart,
With a passion for the game,
And a desire to never fall apart.
    So let us celebrate this game,
Of strategy and skill,
For it brings us all together,
In a way that nothing else will.

Pitching and Fielding

The pitcher stands tall on the mound
With nerves of steel, he looks around
The batter steps up, ready to swing
The game of baseball, an eternal thing
The pitcher winds up, the ball takes flight
As the batter swings with all his might
The fielders watch with bated breath
As the ball soars towards its death
The center fielder races back
As the ball descends on its track
He leaps into the air with grace
And catches the ball in his embrace
The crowd erupts in joyous cheer
As the fielder's catch becomes clear
The pitcher smiles with a sense of pride
As his team's defense takes stride
Baseball is more than just a game
It's a dance of skill and strategy, not just fame

Pitching and fielding, a delicate art
That requires precision and heart
    So let us celebrate this timeless sport
And all the memories it has brought
For on the diamond, anything can occur
In the game of baseball, there's always a lure.

Batting and Base Running

In the field of green, with diamond gleam,
The game of baseball reigns supreme.
With bats in hand and gloves on tight,
The players take their positions to fight.
The pitcher winds up, the ball is thrown,
The batter swings, and the ball is flown.
It soars through the air, high and far,
And lands with a thwack, like a shooting star.
The runner dashes, with all his might,
To first base, where he'll take his flight.
The fielders scramble, the ball in their grasp,
But the runner's safe, with a smile that lasts.
The game goes on, with hits and runs,
The crowd cheers loud, as the players have fun.
The bases are loaded, the tension is high,
As the batter steps up, with a gleam in his eye.
He swings with all his might and main,
And the ball soars high, like a jet plane.

It lands in the stands, with a resounding cheer,
And the batter runs the bases, with no fear.
    The game is won, the players rejoice,
As they high-five and hug, with a unified voice.
For in the game of baseball, it's not just the score,
It's the teamwork, the spirit, and the love of the lore.

The Evolution of Baseball

In fields of green, the game begins,
A bat, a ball, the crowd begins to grin.
The pitcher winds up, the batter takes aim,
A swing and a miss, the game's not the same.
From humble beginnings, the game did grow,
Evolving with time, a new era did show.
Gone are the days of spitballs and dirt,
A sport of precision, a science of work.
From Elysian Fields to modern-day parks,
The game has changed, but still holds its heart.
From Cy Young to Babe Ruth, to modern-day stars,
Baseball's history is etched in the stars.
The crack of the bat, the roar of the crowd,
A timeless sound, heard clear and loud.
From the sandlots to the big leagues,
Baseball's evolution has been a thing to see.
The game still holds its magic, its charm,
A sport that defies time, a game that's not harmed.

A pastime for all, a game of the heart,
Baseball's evolution will never be torn apart.

Robinson, Campanella, and Mays

The crack of the bat, the roar of the crowd
In ballparks across the land, a game once proud
But for years, a divide kept players apart
Black and white, segregated by heart
    Yet in 1947, a brave man took the field
Jackie Robinson, his talent revealed
Breaking the color barrier, history made
Baseball forever changed, a debt unpaid
    No longer would race be a barrier to play
Talent and skill, the only thing to sway
A game once divided, now united as one
A symbol of progress, a job well done
    So let us celebrate the men who paved the way
Robinson, Campanella, and Mays
Their courage and skill, a legacy to behold
A game of baseball, once divided, now bold

Climb and Climb

Baseball, the American pastime,
With attendance records that climb and climb.
From Fenway to Dodger Stadium,
Fans flock to see their team's grand slam.
The crack of the bat, the roar of the crowd,
The excitement of a close game, never allowed to be shroud.
The smell of hot dogs and freshly cut grass,
The feeling of pride when your team takes a pass.
From Cooperstown to the Hall of Fame,
Legends of the game etched in history, earning their claim to fame.
Babe Ruth, Jackie Robinson, and Hank Aaron,
Their records still standing, with fans still cheering on.
Baseball, a game that brings us together,
A sport that will be cherished forever.
From Little League to the Major Leagues,
We'll always love the game and its feats.

The World Stage

On fields of green, with bats and gloves,
The game of baseball, the world it loves.
From Little League to the Major Leagues,
The roar of the crowd, the crack of the tees.
From coast to coast, and across the seas,
The world's united through this game of peace.
No matter the language, culture, or race,
The game of baseball brings us to the same place.
From Tokyo to Havana, and everywhere in between,
The game of baseball creates a global scene.
The World Series, the Olympics, and more,
Baseball's played on a world stage, that's for sure.
So let's play ball, and let's play fair,
Let's show the world how much we care.
For on the diamond, and off it too,
Baseball brings us together, me and you.

No Ticking Tocks

On fields of green and diamond white,
The game of baseball takes its flight.
With bats and balls and gloves in hand,
The players take their rightful stand.

And as they play, the world stands still,
As if time has lost its will.
For in this game, there are no clocks,
No time limits or ticking tocks.

Instead, it's just the players' skill,
Their hits and throws that give the thrill.
The crack of bat, the roar of crowd,
The moments that make baseball proud.

And so we watch for innings nine,
Or maybe more, if we're feeling fine.
For in this game, there's no rush,
No need to hurry, no need to blush.

Just baseball, pure and simple fun,
A game that's loved by everyone.

And even though it has no time,
We'll keep on watching, inning by inning, line by line.

High Batting Average

Bats crack and echo through the air,
As the ball flies without a care.
In the field, the players roam,
Hoping to catch the ball and bring it home.
The pitcher winds up, ready to throw,
His arm a blur, the ball on the go.
The batter waits, eyes on the prize,
Ready to hit it out of the park and rise.
A high batting average is the goal,
A feat that requires skill and control.
Each swing, each hit, brings the chance,
To increase the number and enhance.
Baseball is a game of strategy and might,
Where every player must be ready to fight.
But the one with the highest average of all,
Is the one who will stand tall.
So swing away, and don't hold back,
Hit the ball with all your knack.

For in the game of baseball, it's true,
A high batting average is the key to breakthrough.

The Thrill of Hitting a Home Run

The crowd roars with anticipation,
As the batter steps up to the plate.
The pitcher winds up with determination,
And throws with all his might and weight.
The ball hurtles towards the plate,
As the batter swings with all his might.
The sound of wood hitting leather is great,
And the ball takes off into the night.
The outfielders scramble to catch the ball,
But it's too late, it's already gone.
The batter rounds the bases, standing tall,
As the crowd cheers and sings his song.
The thrill of hitting a home run,
Is like nothing else in the game.
It's a feeling that can't be outdone,
And brings eternal glory and fame.
So swing away, you mighty batters,

And hit that ball out of the park.
For the thrill of hitting a home run matters,
And will forever leave its mark.

Bases Loaded

The pitcher winds up, the batter's ready stance
A flash of movement, the ball's in a trance
It curves and it dips, the batter takes aim
The crowd holds its breath, the tension aflame
The swing is swift, the ball takes to flight
The outfielders scramble, it's a beautiful sight
The bases are loaded, the stakes are high
This hit could make or break the game, oh my!
The ball soars far, over the fence it goes
The batter rounds the bases, his excitement grows
The crowd erupts, the energy's electric
This grand slam hit, it's truly majestic
The players high-five, the dugout cheers
The fans are on their feet, shedding happy tears
Baseball is a game of skill and might
And watching a grand slam is the ultimate delight.

Heroes of the Past

Baseball, a game of heroes past,
Of legends who played it with class.
Their feats on the field, forever to last,
Their passion for the game, unsurpassed.

From Ruth to Aaron, DiMaggio to Paige,
Their names forever etched on the stage.
They played for the love of the game,
Their legacy, a lasting flame.

Their skills with the ball and the glove,
Their dedication, a sight to behold.
Their achievements, a testament to love,
For a game that's worth more than gold.

Baseball, a game of strategy and skill,
Where heroes are made and legends fulfill.
Their stories, a treasure to cherish,
Their impact, forever to nourish.

So let us celebrate these heroes of the past,
Whose love for the game, forever to last.

For baseball, a game that's more than a sport,
But a passion that's worth so much more.

A Perfect Game

The pitcher takes the mound,
His focus sharp and sound,
He stares down the batter,
As the fans all chatter.
The first pitch is thrown,
A strike, the umpire's shown,
The crowd holds its breath,
As the pitcher stares down death.
Inning after inning,
The pitcher keeps on winning,
His throws are precise,
His pitches like dice.
The game is a masterpiece,
As the pitcher's dominance doesn't cease,
His fastball's like a rocket,
His curveball's like a pocket.
The fans watch in awe,
As the pitcher takes them on a draw,

A perfect game pitched,
Their excitement can't be ditched.
    The game of baseball is a wonder,
As the pitcher's skills make it thunder,
A perfect game is a rare sight,
A moment of pure delight.

The Steal

In the diamond, a game is played,
Of strategy and skill, a cunning crusade.
The players run, the bases steal,
A battle of wits, to see who will seal
The victory in this timeless game,
Where every move can bring fame.
The catcher waits, with mitt in hand,
As the runner tries to take a stand.
A blur of motion, a flash of steel,
A stolen base, a chance to feel
The thrill of victory, the agony of defeat,
In this game, where every play is neat.
The pitcher throws, the runner leads,
The crowd sits silent, as the action proceeds.
A quick glance, a dash for home,
The catcher waits, his fate unknown.
The umpire calls, the crowd erupts,
The runner safe, as the pitcher corrupts.

In the game of baseball, the steal is key,
A chance to change the game, to be free.
To outsmart the opponent, to take the lead,
To steal the base, to plant the seed
Of victory in the hearts of all,
In this game, where skill can never fall.

The No-Hitter

The pitcher stands alone on the mound,
With nerves of steel and focus profound,
He stares down each batter with a steely glare,
Determined to keep them all at bay, with no runs to spare.
The ball leaves his hand with finesse and grace,
As it cuts through the air at a breakneck pace,
The batter swings, but it's all in vain,
As the ball flies past, leaving nothing but a stain.
The game is a battle of wits and skill,
As each team strives to gain the upper hand and thrill,
But for the pitcher, it's a test of endurance and might,
To keep the batters guessing and out of sight.
And when the final out is made,
And the pitcher's no-hitter is displayed,
The crowd erupts in a joyous roar,
As they celebrate the triumph of the game's core.
For the no-hitter is a rare feat indeed,
A testament to the pitcher's strength and speed,

And though it may not make a sound,
It's a moment that will forever resound.

| 34 |

The No-Hitter

The pitcher stands alone on the mound,
With nerves of steel and focus profound,
He stares down each batter with a steely glare,
Determined to keep them all at bay, with no runs to spare.
    The ball leaves his hand with finesse and grace,
As it cuts through the air at a breakneck pace,
The batter swings, but it's all in vain,
As the ball flies past, leaving nothing but a stain.
    The game is a battle of wits and skill,
As each team strives to gain the upper hand and thrill,
But for the pitcher, it's a test of endurance and might,
To keep the batters guessing and out of sight.
    And when the final out is made,
And the pitcher's no-hitter is displayed,
The crowd erupts in a joyous roar,
As they celebrate the triumph of the game's core.
    For the no-hitter is a rare feat indeed,
A testament to the pitcher's strength and speed,

And though it may not make a sound,
It's a moment that will forever resound.

Relics and Autographs

The game of baseball, a timeless classic,
With players skilled and fierce and fantastic.
The thrill of the pitch, the swing of the bat,
The joy of victory, the sting of defeat, all that.
But beyond the field, a hobby so dear,
Collecting baseball cards, year after year.
From rookie cards to relics and autographs,
The thrill of the hunt, the joy of the catch.
Trading with friends, the excitement of a find,
The memories of games, forever enshrined.
A game within a game, a passion so true,
Baseball and collecting, forever intertwined.
So here's to America's pastime, and the cards we hold dear,
A tradition that will always persevere.

Beautiful Ballparks

The smell of grass, the taste of hot dogs,
The sights and sounds of the game,
Each ballpark unique, its own charm,
A place where memories are made.
From the ivy walls of Wrigley,
To the Green Monster at Fenway,
The charm of old Yankee Stadium,
To the modern marvel of Petco Park.
The hum of the organ at Dodger Stadium,
The train whistle at Minute Maid,
Each ballpark a living museum,
A place where history is made.
The roar of the crowd, the crack of the bat,
All part of the game we love,
But it's the ballparks across the country,
That make it a treasure trove.
So come and visit the ballparks,
From coast to coast and more,

And experience the magic of baseball,
Like never before.

The World Series

The diamond gleams beneath the lights
As players take their place
The pitcher stares down home plate
With a fierce and steady face
    The game begins, the tension high
As every play unfolds
Each team fighting tooth and nail
To reach their final goals
    The World Series is on the line
A title to be won
The victor will go down in lore
The loser, all but done
The ball is hit, it soars up high
The fielders give their chase
The crowd holds its collective breath
As they await the fate
    The game is close, the innings pass
The tension mounting still

The players know they're on the brink
And give it all their will
    And then it's over, just like that
The victors take their place
The World Series champions crowned
In this timeless baseball race

Sabermetrics

The players take the field with grace,
Their stats and skills put to the test.
A game of strategy, not just pace,
Sabermetrics, the key to success.

Numbers and data, the heart of the game,
A science that's changed how we play.
The past is no longer the same,
The future lies in what stats say.

From on-base percentage to WAR,
Each metric tells a story untold.
Gone are the days of gut feel and lore,
Sabermetrics, the new gold.

A game of inches, a game of wits,
Sabermetrics, a tool to survive.
Innovations that have changed the bits,
Of a game that's more than just alive.

So bring on the stats, the metrics galore,
Let the numbers tell the tale.

For in this game, we can't ignore,
The power of sabermetrics to prevail.

The Walk-Off Win

The crowd is on their feet,
Tension fills the air
The game is on the line,
A walk-off is near
    The pitcher takes his stance,
Aiming for the plate
The batter digs in deep,
Ready to seal his fate
    The first pitch is a strike,
The second's fouled away
The third pitch comes in hot,
But the batter won't sway
He connects with the ball,
It soars through the sky
The outfielders give chase,
But it's just too high
    The ball clears the fence,
The crowd erupts in cheers

The batter rounds the bases,
Overwhelmed by the cheers
    The walk-off is complete,
The game is finally won
The thrill of victory,
A feeling like no other one.

Rock Your World

The crack of the bat, the roar of the crowd,
The game of baseball is played loud and proud.
From the pitcher's mound, the ball is hurled,
At speeds so great, it can rock your world.
The 100 miles per hour fastball,
Is a thing of beauty, a sight to behold.
It whizzes past, like a speeding train,
And leaves the batter feeling quite insane.
The pitcher's wind up, the tension builds,
The batter stares down, his eyes filled with will.
The ball is released, a blur in the air,
The batter swings hard, but it's all despair.
The umpire calls, the pitch a strike,
The batter shakes his head, it's not his night.
But the pitcher grins, he knows he's boss,
And he'll keep throwing heat, no matter the cost.
Baseball is a game of skill and might,
Where the fastball reigns supreme in the night.

So if you're a fan, or just passing by,
Take a moment to appreciate the fastball fly.

Spring Training

The crack of the bat, the smell of the grass
Spring training time has come at last
Players take the field, ready to play
Preparing for the season, day by day
The sun shines bright, the sky so blue
As they practice and train, each player anew
Pitchers throw fastballs, curveballs and more
Fielders catch pop-ups, grounders and soar
The fans gather 'round, excitement in the air
Watching their favorite players, without a care
The game of baseball, a timeless tradition
Spring training the start, with no inhibition
As the season draws near, the teams take flight
Ready to compete, with all their might
The game of baseball, a true work of art
Spring training the beginning, playing a part
So let's cheer on our teams, as they take the field
With every hit and pitch, their fate is sealed

The game of baseball, a thing of beauty
Spring training the start, fulfilling duty.

The Bull-Pen Warm Up

The sun beats down on the diamond green
As players take their spots, a familiar scene
But in a corner, away from the fray
Pitchers warm up, getting ready to play
In the bull-pen, they toss the ball
A dance with gravity, a curve, a crawl
Each pitch a symphony, a work of art
A prelude to the game about to start
The crack of the bat, the roar of the crowd
The pitcher's heart beats, but he stands proud
For he knows he's prepared, he's done his part
His time has come, to take heart
So let the game begin, let it unfold
The pitcher's arm, strong and bold
Let the ball fly, fast and true
And let us see what he can do.

Baseball and Anthem

The sun sets on the diamond,
the field is all aglow,
The players take their places,
and the crowd begins to grow.
The umpire calls "Play Ball!",
and the game begins to start,
The pitcher winds up his arm,
and the batter takes his part.
The crack of the bat, the roar of the crowd,
the ball soaring high and far,
The players run the bases,
each one like a shooting star.
But before the game can start,
there's a moment to recall,
The national anthem is played,
and the players stand tall.
With hands on hearts, they listen,
to the anthem's stirring sound,

As they think of all the heroes,
who fought and stood their ground.
    And as the anthem fades away,
the players take their place,
Ready to play the game they love,
with pride and skill and grace.
    Baseball and anthem, a perfect pair,
a tribute to the land we love,
And as we cheer our team to victory,
we honor those above.

Baseball and Seeds

Baseball and sunflower seeds,
A perfect combination that meets all our needs,
As we sit in the stands and watch the game,
We chew on seeds and cheer with aim.

The crack of the bat, the roar of the crowd,
The sunflower seeds, the gum we chow,
As we root for our favorite team,
We munch away and live the dream.

The pitcher winds up, the batter swings,
We spit out shells and do our things,
The game of baseball, a true delight,
As we chew and spit into the night.

So let's enjoy this game we love,
With sunflower seeds and gum to shove,
For baseball and these tasty treats,
Are a match made in heaven, can't be beat.

Them Dogs

In the field of green, the game's begun,
The crowds are cheering, it's all in fun.
The pitcher winds up, throws the ball,
The batter swings, aiming for it all.
    The hot dog vendor walks the stands,
Selling franks with mustard in his hands.
The fans all munch, enjoying the game,
Hoping for glory, fortune, and fame.
    The outfielders run, chasing the ball,
Trying to catch it before it falls.
The umpire calls, "Strike one, two, three!",
The tension builds, who will it be?
As the innings pass, the sun sets low,
The score is tied, it's time to go.
The final pitch, the crowd holds its breath,
Will it be victory or sudden death?
    The ball is hit, it's flying high,
The outfielder races, so close to the sky.

He jumps and catches, the game is done,
The crowd erupts, a victory won.
	The hot dog vendor packs his cart,
The fans all cheer with all their heart.
Baseball and hot dogs, a perfect pair,
A timeless tradition, we'll always share.

The Catcher

The field is green, the sky is blue,
The catcher crouches, ready to do
His job behind the plate, so crucial and key,
To catch every pitch with skill and agility.
With gear and mask, he's a warrior in battle,
Calling the shots, his mind sharp as a rattle,
He's the catcher, the commander, the heart of the team,
The one who keeps them together, like a well-oiled machine.
He blocks the ball, he throws to the base,
He's the one who keeps the runners in their place,
He's the catcher, the guardian of home,
The one who makes sure the opponents don't roam.
So here's to the catcher, the unsung hero of the game,
The one who plays with heart and never seeks fame,
He's the backbone of the team, the glue that holds it tight,
The catcher, the warrior, the shining light.

First Base

On the diamond, a warrior's quest,
A battle of skill and strength, no rest.
The ball is thrown, the runner flies,
The crowd erupts in cheers and cries.

At first base, a guardian stands,
Commander of the infield lands.
A beacon of hope, a steadfast guide,
The backbone of the team's pride.

With nimble footwork and steady hand,
The first baseman guards the land.
A wall of defense, a force to reckon,
The shining light, the team's beacon.

In this game of strategy and might,
The first baseman shines so bright.
A hero unsung, a role so crucial,
Their value to the team, truly special.

So let us honor the first base,
Their skill and strength, their noble grace.

For in this game of baseball lore,
The first baseman's role we must adore.

Shortstop

The shortstop stands with poised grace,
Gazing out at the diamond's expanse.
His mind sharp, his eyes fixed,
Ready for any ball to chance.
The game of baseball is his life,
His passion, his love, his all.
He guards his base with fierce pride,
Ever ready to answer the call.
With every catch, every throw,
He solidifies his place in the game.
The shortstop, a true field leader,
A hero with a noble name.
So here's to the shortstop,
A vital part of the team.
May he always stand strong and true,
And forever chase the diamond dream.

Center Field

In center field, he stands alone,
His eyes fixed on the pitcher's throne.
The roar of fans, the smell of grass,
He waits for the ball to pass.
His glove held high, he's ready to go,
To catch the ball, a hero's role.
He waits for the signal, the pitch is thrown,
He runs and leaps, the ball is flown.
Outstretched arms, he makes the catch,
The crowd erupts, their cheers attach.
A moment of glory, a moment of pride,
In center field, he takes it all in stride.
A game of strategy, a game of skill,
In center field, he plays with will.
The sun beats down, the wind does blow,
But he's determined, he won't let go.
In center field, he's always in sight,
A beacon of hope, a shining light.

For his team, he'll do what it takes,
In center field, he'll make no mistakes.

Second Base

When the game of baseball is in full swing,
And the crowd is cheering with everything,
A player on second base is a sight to behold,
Ready to run, steal, or be bold.
With a keen eye and a quick mind,
He watches the pitcher, waiting for the sign,
Then takes off with a burst of speed,
Sliding into second with graceful ease.
The fielders scramble to make the play,
But the player on second is here to stay,
A strategic position, he holds the key,
To scoring runs and victory.
So here's to second base, the unsung hero,
Who makes the game of baseball a true spectacle,
A position of skill, grace, and might,
That shines brightly in the stadium lights.

Right Field

In the game of baseball, right field is where I stand,
Glove in hand, ready to catch whatever comes to land.
The sun beats down, it's a scorching hot day,
But I'm focused on the game, ready to play.
The ball comes flying, soaring through the air,
I run towards it, without a care.
My heart pounds, as I reach out my hand,
And make the catch, as if it were planned.
The crowd roars, as I toss the ball back,
Feeling proud, with nothing to lack.
In right field, I'll always be,
A key player, for all to see.
So here I stand, in my rightful place,
Ready to play, with skill and grace.
The game of baseball, a true delight,
And in right field, I shine so bright.

America's Pastime

Baseball, America's pastime
A game of strategy and skill
Played on fields of green
Where legends are made and heroes thrill
From the crack of the bat
To the roar of the crowd
There's nothing quite like
The game that makes us proud
The pitcher on the mound
With a ball in his hand
Ready to throw a strike
And make the batter stand
The crack of the bat
As the ball takes flight
It's a moment of beauty
A true delight
The outfielders running
To catch the ball in flight

Trying to make the play
And end the inning right
　　The game of baseball
Brings us together
To cheer on our team
Through any kind of weather
　　So let us all gather
In this great American tradition
To watch the game we love
And celebrate our nation's ambition

The Love

In love with the game of baseball,
I stand here with my bat,
As the pitcher winds up, I'm ready,
For that perfect pitch to splat.
The crack of the bat, the roar of the crowd,
A home run hit, I'm proud,
Running the bases, heart racing,
In love with the game, I am astounded.
The smell of the grass, the feel of the sun,
Playing the game is so much fun,
From little league to the majors,
I'll never stop, I'm a true ball player.
In love with the game of baseball,
It's more than just a sport,
It's a way of life, a passion,
Forever in my heart, it will be caught.

Walter the Educator is one of the pseudonyms for Walter Anderson. Formally educated in Chemistry, Business, and Education, he is an educator, an author, a diverse entrepreneur, and the son of a disabled war veteran. "Walter the Educator" shares his time between educating and creating. He holds interests and owns several creative projects that entertain, enlighten, enhance, and educate, hoping to inspire and motivate you.

WaltertheEducator.com